GW01466407

Dorset Library Service

- Please return items by the last date shown on this label, or on your self-service receipt.
- Renew books by phoning 01305 224311 or online www.librarieswest.org.uk
- Items may be returned to any Dorset library.

Dorset Council

Level 11 – Lime

Helpful Hints for Reading at Home

The graphemes (written letters) and phonemes (units of sound) used throughout this series are aligned with **Letters and Sounds.** This offers a consistent approach to learning whether reading at home or in the classroom.

HERE ARE SOME COMMON WORDS THAT YOUR CHILD MIGHT FIND TRICKY:

water	where	would	know	thought	through	couldn't
laughed	eyes	once	we're	school	can't	our

TOP TIPS FOR HELPING YOUR CHILD TO READ:

- Encourage your child to read aloud as well as silently to themselves.
- Allow your child time to absorb the text and make comments.
- Ask simple questions about the text to assess understanding.
- Encourage your child to clarify the meaning of new vocabulary.

This book focuses on developing independence, fluency and comprehension. It is a lime level 11 book band.

Nathan Chase
in
Thunder
Chase

Written by
Robin Twiddy

Illustrated by
Kris Jones

Chapter One

Don't Go Chasing Laser Beams

Like always, Nathan was playing laser tag. Nathan loved laser tag. He played every Saturday morning and he was good at it. He strapped on his sensor and hefted the laser in his hand. The weight felt good. Nathan stepped into the dark and the horn sounded to start the game.

Nathan ran from pillar to pillar, taking cover and firing off a few shots in the direction of the other team. Soon there were lasers flying all over the place. Nathan found himself ducking behind a chest completely pinned.

"These guys are serious. I think they even brought their own lasers!" thought Nathan, when out of nowhere sprang a man dressed in an expensive-looking tuxedo. He moved like a cat, weaving between lasers. Then, POW! A wooden wall behind Nathan exploded as a laser hit it.

"They're real!" Nathan said out loud. The man in the tuxedo kicked off a wall, flipped over a laser and slid across the floor, coming to rest right next to Nathan.

"Jack Masters," came a voice from the darkness. "There is no escape. Hand over the device." The man turned to Nathan. "Hey kid, take this," he said, handing Nathan his watch. "It is really important that you get that watch to RADAR. Give it to Foxley – no one else. He will know what to do!"

Jack Masters glanced around the laser tag arena before ducking down again. "I am going to distract them. When they come for me, you run for the emergency exit," he said, pointing.

Jack leapt up and narrowly dodged a laser beam. "I didn't know ninja stood for Nincompoops In Nana's Jumpers Alert, but here you are!"

That moment, several figures dressed in blue came out from the shadows and leapt at Jack in a flurry of kicks and punches. "Go, now," he said under his breath. The next thing Nathan knew, he was running.

Chapter Two

The Chase is On

Nathan ran until he was home. It was hard to believe that any of what had just happened was real. If it wasn't for the watch, he probably wouldn't have believed it. Nathan made up his mind – he was going to hide the watch in his treehouse.

Nathan was about to hide the watch when it came to life in his hand. "Kkkrtzzztch... Jack... krtzzztch... Jack are you there..." Nathan almost dropped the watch, but then it lit up again. "Jack, you activated the tracking device, are you in trouble?"

Nathan squinted at the watch. He could see a face staring back at him. "You're not Jack! Who are you?"

"My name is Nathan," said Nathan. "Jack... That must be the name of the man in the tuxedo," he thought to himself.

The face on the screen was older. "You are not supposed to have this watch, my lad," it said.

"Look," replied Nathan. "The man who gave me this watch said it was very important. He said I wasn't supposed to give it to anyone but..." Nathan stopped himself before he said the name.

KRACKABOOM

"Good man!" said the face on the screen. "Looks like Jack gave the watch to the right person. Now let's start again, shall we? My name is Foxley, I am the commander of RADAR. That stands for Rebel Agents Defending Against RUIN. We protect the world from the villainous RUIN."

RUIN WORLD WIDE THREAT LEVEL DEFCON 6

"Jack said I should give the watch to you. I don't want it, especially if it comes with ninjas," Nathan said.

"I'm afraid it's not that simple," Foxley replied. "That watch contains a computer virus. It is the only thing that can stop the storm-cannon, a device designed by RUIN's top scientists. It creates a storm that can tear cities apart and bring the world's governments to their knees."

"What can I do?" asked Nathan.

"Get the watch to me and we can upload the virus to our computers and send it directly to the storm-cannon," Foxley said.
"The watch is a smart watch," he continued. "It is really smart. It has state-of-the-art artificial intelligence. I have instructed it to accept you as its master. It will help you..."
Just then, Foxley was interrupted by a huge crash of thunder.

Nathan had never heard anything that loud before.

"They have activated the device, you must hurry. Good luck and trust no one. RUIN have agents everywhere!" With that said, Foxley was gone and Nathan was alone in his treehouse. Or was he?

Above his head he heard a slight creak as if someone was on the roof of the treehouse.

Nathan saw movement near the door and dashed to the rear window. As he leapt to the grass below, he heard a voice from the treehouse.

"Stop!" shouted the ninja. "Give me that watch and I will let you go free."

Nathan didn't need to know that this guy was a member of an evil secret society to know not to trust him.

He grabbed his bike and headed out the gate.

Nathan peddled like he had never peddled before. He didn't know where he was going but he knew he couldn't stay here.

Behind him he heard the ninja scream, "Get him!"

Figures appeared across the roofs of the surrounding buildings. As Nathan whizzed through the streets, he looked down at the watch.

"Oh well, here goes," he thought to himself. "Watch, help me get out of here."

To Nathan's surprise, the watch lit up and a robotic voice replied. "Hello Nathan, I am OCT347-X, but you can call me Zero. How can I help?"

Above his head, thick black clouds moved across the sky at unnatural speeds, gathering right above him. The wind picked up and the light dimmed as the clouds began to blot out the Sun.

"Get me out of here, I am being chased by ninjas," Nathan shouted over the wind.

"Hold tight Mr Chase, I think you will like this!" said the robotic voice of Zero.

Thin smoke-like stuff came from the watch and started to gather around his bike. "What is that?" Nathan asked.

"Those are nanobots – they are tiny computers, Mr Chase," Zero replied. "They will upgrade your bike."

The bike transformed under him, growing new parts that looked like rocket boosters.

Just then, a beam of light flashed past his face and hit a post box, freezing it solid. Looking back, he could see a ninja on a skateboard just behind him with a futuristic weapon in his hand. "Oh great, freeze-ray carrying skateboarding ninjas. Can this day get any weirder?" Nathan thought.

"Give me the watch, Chase! Or the storm-cannon will tear this town apart," the skateboarding ninja hissed.

Nathan hit the button that the nanobots had added to his bike. His speed doubled in seconds. The world around him started to blur. Then the bike rose off the ground. "I'm flying!" he whooped, as he lifted further into the air. On the ground the ninjas looked like army ants – small and insignificant.

ZOOOM

Chapter Three

A Break from the Chase

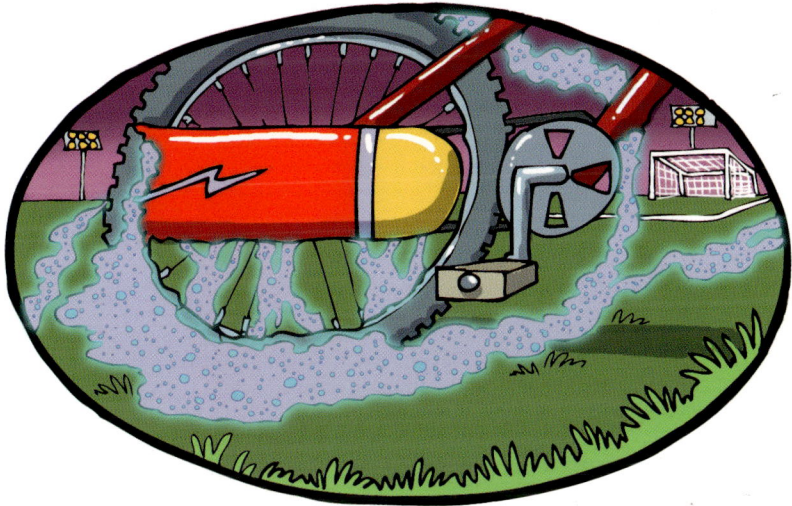

Nathan landed in a playing field not far from the shopping centre. A mist seemed to lift off his bike and whip back into the watch. His bike looked just as it had before.

Tapping the watch on his wrist, Nathan said, "Zero, what do we do now? RUIN is going to destroy my town and then the world if we don't get you to Foxley fast!"

"Well sir, we have around one hour before the storm builds up enough to tear apart the town. I would suggest you contact Foxley again," said Zero. "But unfortunately, this storm is interfering with my ability to send and receive communications," he went on. "We will need to get to higher ground."

"I know just the place," Nathan said. "Saint's Hill. It is just the other side of the shopping centre. Do that thing with the bike again and we'll be there in minutes."

Zero responded, "I am afraid, sir, that the nanobots need to recharge. They will not be available for six hours."

"Oh, then I guess I will use my bike the old-fashioned way," Nathan said, picking the bike up which promptly fell to pieces. "Or walk."

Chapter Four

Thunder Chase

As Nathan stepped into the Saint's Hill Shopping Centre, Foxley's words echoed in his mind: "Good luck and trust no one. RUIN have agents everywhere!" Could these happy shoppers really be agents of RUIN? The world had gone mad. Yesterday he was just another kid who loved to play laser tag, now he was on a mission to save the world. Zero's voice broke this train of thought.

"We have forty-five minutes until the town is destroyed and then only another three hours before the rest of the world follows. You had better hurry," Zero said.

Nathan walked faster. The shopping centre wasn't big, but it would take him ten minutes to get out the other side and then another five to climb the hill. Who knew if Foxley would even receive the call?

It was an indoor shopping centre. The people inside hadn't noticed the violent storm outside until a loud clap of thunder shook the glass ceiling. Suddenly a voice cut through the crowd. It was Mrs Marsh the dinner lady.

"Hi, Miss," Nathan said. "I can't really stop; I am on the clock you could say!"
Nathan turned to walk off, but Mrs Marsh caught hold of his arm. "That's an interesting watch," she said. "Where did you get it?"
"From a friend," Nathan said, now aware of how tight her grip on his arm was.
"Can I have a look?" she asked.

Trust no one. That was what Foxley had said.

"Miss, I really must go," Nathan said. "I am late for something. Can you let go of my arm please?"

Mrs Marsh didn't let go, but she did smile.

"RUIN!" Nathan said under his breath.

"That's right," said the dinner lady. "You are coming with me."

"I don't think so..." Nathan said. "Zero, help!"

"Yes, sir," the watch replied. Suddenly, a
beam shot out from it and hit the dinner lady.
She froze on the spot. Nathan pulled his arm
free and said, "I will stop this storm, and I
will stop RUIN!" The evil dinner lady couldn't
move, but she could speak.
"He's here!" she screamed.

Nathan ran. He saw a little old lady pull a
rather large weapon out of her shopping bag.
A shop assistant then dropped a pile of books
and pulled a blaster of some type from his
belt. "Crikey," he thought. The air above his
head filled with streaming lights.

Nathan saw one of the blasts hit a balloon. It turned to ice and fell to the floor in pieces. "At least they are only shooting freeze rays," Nathan thought to himself.

Soon, there was only Nathan and the agents of RUIN left in the building. Nathan dived for cover behind a bin.

"Zero, what can I do?" Nathan asked desperately.

"As you saw with Mrs Marsh, I am capable of firing a non-lethal stun ray. Just point your arm at the target and clench your fist to fire," said the smart watch. "I am afraid that is all I can do to help until my nanobots are fully charged."

"Okay, here goes nothing," Nathan said to himself. He spotted the exit – it was twenty metres away. He could make it if he ran fast. Nathan dived over a bench. He spotted two agents between him and the door.

All those years of laser tag hadn't been wasted. Nathan was fast and smooth. He moved like lightning. Dodging blasts fired at him with a duck and a spin, he clenched his fist and the first of them froze to the spot.

He twisted, adjusted his aim and fired again. The second, who had been running when Nathan fired, was now frozen stiff, balanced on one foot. He wobbled for a second before toppling over.

Whizz. A blast flew past Nathan's ear.

Lightning struck the glass ceiling and it shattered above the agents that were chasing him. They dived for cover.

Knowing this was his chance, Nathan ran for the door, the wind now whistling through the gaping hole in the ceiling. He threw himself out of the exit and into the storm outside. He charged up the stairs leading up the hill. The wind made it like running under water. Behind him, the last two RUIN agents were making their way up the steps. They had been joined by three RUIN ninjas.

"Zero, send the signal!" Nathan screamed over the howling wind.

The agents of RUIN made it to the top of the hill seconds behind him. "Nathan, stop!" shouted the ninja from before. He recognised that voice. Even when he stood still, the wind was strong enough to push him across the wet grass. He grabbed hold of the statue of the saint.

"It is too late for you, boy!" said the ninja, who pulled out a dagger and dug it into the ground to stop himself from being torn away by the rising storm. The other agents of RUIN were not as smart as the first ninja. Without anything to hold on to, they were swept away by the storm.

The ninja edged closer to Nathan, little by little. There was nowhere to run. If Nathan let go of the statue, he would face the same fate as the agents of RUIN. It was only a matter of time before the ninja was upon him.

A bright light cut through the darkness and a man in heavy iron boots dropped between Nathan and the ninja. It was Jack Masters. "Thanks kid, you did a great job. I'll take it from here. Foxley is waiting for you," he said. A rope dropped in front of Nathan and he was quickly hauled into a waiting helicopter.

Foxley stood in the helicopter next to a computer panel. "Quick, kid. The watch."

Nathan handed it over and Foxley plugged it in. A few quick taps on the panel and signal was sent. The sky began to clear.

"That will do it," said Foxley. "Let's give Jack a hand. Land the chopper," he called through to the cockpit.

When they landed Jack stood with the ninja unconscious at his feet. His tuxedo was still pristine despite the storm and the fight.

"Well Nathan, you really came through for us," Jack said. "I knew I could escape RUIN but I wasn't sure if I would have made it out with the watch intact."

"Thanks," Nathan said, trying to catch his breath.

"What are your plans for Saturday morning?" Foxley asked.

"What?" Nathan replied, confused by the question.

"Well, make sure you are free. Training begins at 08:00 am," Foxley said. "We will send a chopper." Then he tossed Nathan the watch. "Better keep hold of that, you might need it."

Nathan caught the watch and strapped it on to his wrist. He looked out over the town. Despite some damage it looked like he had managed to save the day just in time.

Jack Masters punched him on the shoulder and said, "Nathan Chase agent of RADAR. Got a nice ring to it, eh!"

Nathan Chase in Thunder Chase

1. What is Nathan doing when he first meets Jack Masters?

2. What is the name of the watch?

3. What is the device made by RUIN?

    a) Storm-cannon

    b) Fire sword

    c) Spider bomb

4. What did the nanobots do to Nathan's bike?

5. Will Nathan be a good RADAR agent? Would you want to be a RADAR agent?

BookLife
PUBLISHING

BookLife
Readers

©2021 **BookLife Publishing Ltd.**
King's Lynn, Norfolk PE30 4LS

ISBN 978–1–83927–414–5

Nathan Chase In Thunder Chase
Written by Robin Twiddy
Illustrated by Kris Jones

An Introduction to BookLife Readers...

Our Readers have been specifically created in line with the London Institute of Education's approach to book banding and are phonetically decodable and ordered to support each phase of Letters and Sounds.

Each book has been created to provide the best possible reading and learning experience. Our aim is to share our love of books with children, providing both emerging readers and prolific page-turners with beautiful books that are guaranteed to provoke interest and learning, regardless of ability.

BOOK BAND GRADED using the Institute of Education's approach to levelling.

PHONETICALLY DECODABLE supporting each phase of Letters and Sounds.

EXERCISES AND QUESTIONS to offer reinforcement and to ascertain comprehension.

BEAUTIFULLY ILLUSTRATED to inspire and provoke engagement, providing a variety of styles for the reader to enjoy whilst reading through the series.

AUTHOR INSIGHT:
ROBIN TWIDDY

Robin Twiddy is one of BookLife Publishing's most creative and prolific editorial talents, who imbues all his copy with a sense of adventure and energy. Robin's Cambridge-based first class honours degree in psychosocial studies offers a unique viewpoint on factual information and allows him to relay information in a manner that readers of any age are guaranteed to retain. He also holds a certificate in Teaching in the Lifelong Sector, and a post graduate certificate in Consumer Psychology.

A father of two, Robin has written over 70 titles for BookLife and specialises in conceptual, role-playing narratives which promote interaction with the reader and inspire even the most reluctant of readers to fully engage with his books.

This book focuses on developing independence, fluency and comprehension. It is a lime level 11 book band.